What I tell myself at night

Palewell Press

What I tell myself at night

Poems about loss and letting go

Camilla Reeve

What I tell myself at night

First edition 2022 from Palewell Press, www.palewellpress.co.uk

Printed and bound in the UK

ISBN 978-1-911587-54-5

All Rights Reserved. Copyright © 2022 Camilla Reeve. No part of this publication may be reproduced or transmitted in any form or by any means, without permission in writing from the author. The right of Camilla Reeve to be identified as the author of this work has been asserted by her in accordance with the Copyright, Designs and Patents Act 1988

The cover design is Copyright © 2022 Camilla Reeve

The front cover image is Copyright © 2022 Tom Harding

The back cover photo is Copyright © 2022 Camilla Reeve

A CIP catalogue record for this title is available from the British Library.

Acknowledgements

Enormous thanks to Tom Harding, www.tomharding.net – poet, illustrator and friend – for this collection's front cover image.

Thanks very much to my writing buddies – Christie Dickason, who edited the collection, and to Jane Sherwin, Jenny Messer, Margaret Whittock, Kathleen Cornelia and Alwyn Marriage who provided feedback on individual poems.

An earlier version of the poem "Bidey-In" first appeared in *These we have loved* – Wordshare Poets anthology, 2017.

Dedication

For my darling Oz, 1959-2020. Thank you for everything and, especially, for being so supportive of my writing.

You were my port in a storm,
my rock of certainty,
my deep-sea trench of shared silence,
my whale-song of yearning
and my porpoise-leap of joy.

Contents

BEFOREHAND	1
Leaping Luminescence	2
Croatia – Terracotta Roof	4
Croatia – Wild Swimming Near Zadar	6
Bidey-In	7
Feeling empty	8
Listen	9
SHIELDING	11
Remember, remember the 5th of November…	12
Afternoon rest	13
Not listening	14
Away	15
Demise	16
Silence	17
Gone are the days	18
Not falling	19
Beloved	20
Fairy-lighted time	22
The Hug	23
Navigation	24
Your last weeks	25
Holding Hands	26
Metamorphosis	27

BEREAVED	29
What I tell myself at night…	30
Invisible Friend	32
I planted runner beans…	33
Freezing Beans	34
Guilt	36
Don't say it	37
Clearing out your car	38
Raspberries in November	39
Looking forward	40
Wizard in the shed	41
My loss	42
Something I don't know	43
AFTER-KNOWLEDGE	45
A widow's words to her counsellor	46
Hindsight	48
My bedroom…	49
Goodbye	50
Phone call from a friend	52
Your turn to cook	54
Six months on	55
Whereabouts unknown	56
A year of getting ready…	57
Moving Day	58
When I'm ready	59

Go on, fill your boots!	60
St Bees Beach	62
CAMILLA REEVE - BIOGRAPHY	64

BEFOREHAND

Leaping Luminescence

To be with you,
our last free evening.
Dusk fades to night.
Light blurs across the water.
Fish are leaping, radiant,
from hidden to visible
then lost again.

To be with you:
a special meal,
begun with olives,
bread and wine.
A waiter hovers
then draws back
into pillared shadows.

In the pool
beside our table
fish cruise the depths,
are known about,
unseen, imagined,
leap for insects,
luminesce.

You and I talk
about what's happened,
what may come one day,
not thinking
what we ought to say,
only what we want
and need to share,

a dozen unimportant
snippets of conversation
skim hidden depths:
our own radiance;
our leaps apart
then side by side,
apart then one again.

This meal together,
dark waters at our side,
dark sky above,
acknowledging
our pillared shadows,
the darting hours and
flowing years of love.

Croatia – Terracotta Roof

Loving the tiled roof opposite our hotel room…

because she's beautiful;
her faded terracotta hits a shade
halfway from orange-peel to pine-tree trunk,
recalling that trip south at twenty-one
with my best cousin-friend for company,
on hillsides redolent with thyme, the red wine drunk,
and having time ahead to do things with,
so much of it that spending days being chased
by boys we'd never see again was not a waste
but youth and making hay;

because she's old
like painted skies inside cathedral domes
complete with stars and cherubs, or the wheels
preserved from chariots that raced the Coliseum,
or little streets with laundry strung across them
and flower-filled balconies, where houses lean
so close they might be gossiping, and all the skills
that master craftsmen learned and taught
till factory-culture stole our joy from making things,
as old as these at least;

because she's broken
cracked and out of true. On one row
every tile has snapped in two,
weeds pushing through the gaps.
Her brokenness is like my own—
not totally unuseful yet
but less complete, less beautiful,
less of the pride I used to have in things,
still here though and, on balance,
functioning…

              I think perhaps
the roof and I have caught each other
before too many tiles have fallen
onto the courtyard floor
and smashed beyond all mending.
So until then, why worry, why repair?
This ageing roof still has a job to do
and does it well.

Croatia – Wild Swimming Near Zadar

Eyes bright as raindrops, sparrows dive from bushes,
shrill voices calling as they hawk for insects.

Below them, there's a slithering of lizards.
Improbably long tongues flick in and out.
Green torso'd bodies dart from rock to rock
on sand still damp from last night's downpour.

While I screw up my nerve to try
wild swimming in a sea that's rough but warm
the bending branches of a parasol pine
drip resin on my shorts and shirt. I smile.

Some moments hold such happiness we brim with it
until we're swimming through the universe.

Bidey-In

Because you have been willing
to stand outside on windy nights
bearing a basket of wet sheets
and waiting while I hang them out –

my shape against the passing clouds
no clearer than yours is to me
yet truly as our own reflections
we know each other's silhouette –

and, even as you heft the basket,
you tease me for not wearing shoes
and risking bruises from the stones
and how I'd scold *your* shoelessness.

We laugh about my bossiness,
your lack of time for household tasks,
why two such very different humans
would hate to live or sleep apart,

and for the sum of all these parts
and other joys too deep to name
you are my dear abiding love
and bide within my heart.

Footnote: *"Bidey-In" is a Scottish term for a live-in lover*

Feeling empty

You're sleeping in a hotel room
hundreds of miles away.
I wander through our empty house—
Marie Celeste with you the missing crew.

Our goodnight call's behind me,
back upon the riverbank of evening,
an act I try not to reprise
except in an emergency.

I know just where you are,
told you to please drive carefully,
kissed you before you left,
all good-luck boxes have been ticked.

Even so, on entering our room,
empty of your stuff
your side of our big bed untenanted
I'm feeling empty too.

Listen

For a time, life goes on
as you've always known it,
are in the way of getting to know it,
each new thing slowly –
new job, new route to work,
new friend to buy your lunch with,
and letting go of other things –
old job, a previous partner,
views you used to hold.

Only then
something happens,
something you didn't anticipate,
no really, didn't ever think would come along.

It may appear quite small –
a skid of pebbles rolling down a beach,
an unfamiliar sound on your commute,
strangers you see stumble away
from dust-clouds, gold against the sun,
but your body knows, tenses itself to run
and your mind agrees but where to run
when what has happened is unlike
anything imagined?

So you freeze,
as still as shaking knees
and clenching fists allow
and listen.

SHIELDING

Remember, remember the 5th of November…

as if I'm ever likely to forget
though what will be remembered I don't know

outside the sky lights up with rockets
and shooting stars all colours of the rainbow

but one great firework, hidden in my heart,
has yet to detonate

I'm holding what you said close to my chest,
so close it's hard to breathe –

details from your Clinical Nurse Practitioner,
painstaking forecasts of your future pain –

when will your gift of gunpowder explode,
when will my calm be blown apart and lost?

Afternoon rest

My darling,
lie back on your old chair and have a sleep
head bending sideways like a bird at rest
between one long migration and the next.
Meanwhile I let myself peer through the gate
and far enough away to see and feel
what may, although I hope not, lie in wait;
let myself for a handful of brave moments,
though maybe they are also foolish ones,
believe in that sad future and, believing,
capture a photo of you safe asleep,
a picture of this time before life changes
with body and mind still functioning as one,
when you can think to raise a hand and it will rise
or to restrain a cry and it stays silent.
I will not share this photo with you,
don't dare to risk a chance of saying
I gazed into that maybe-time before
our days and circumstances forced me to
and, like Lot's wife, fear I precipitated
what otherwise might not have come to pass.

Not listening

While you still listen
you'll find that people tell you things.
Doctors, for instance,

say we should sleep in separate beds,
that you should eat more protein,
not look too far ahead.

They're only passing on what helped
millions of other patients
but you're unique and precious.

Friends follow up their stares
of shock and sorrow
with tales of someone else's cure.

What do they know?
Not what would really comfort me—
if they could fix tomorrow

or cauterize my feelings.
But that's alright, you see –
I just stopped listening.

Away

Won't you come home, Bill Bailey,
Won't you come home?
           Of course, you are at home, for now.

There was me believing the trouble was
you working far away, and only home
for each two-day weekend

then gone again to a Midlands town
I'd never get to know
with its rows of factories and roofs.

Fool that I was not relishing
my life with two whole days of you
more or less every week.

As you rest, your breath
comes and goes so slowly
I dig my nails into my palms

to stop myself from checking
whether you're still breathing
or if this time of tests

and waiting and more tests
is just a waking dream
and you've already gone…
gone away, Bill Bailey.

Demise

I've never known the way to say
the word that's spelt d-e-m-i-s-e.

Should it be rhymed with prize
for a battle that was bravely won

or with surprise about
the end that came so suddenly,

or should the sound resemble ease,
much longed-for after battling disease,

or please – let all of it be over soon
and him not suffer any longer –

but not forgetting my half-life of a thousand years
in which it half-rhymes with bereave and grieve.

Silence

You tell me bleeding has begun again
from the same place, this time before the op
not after it. Now I am caught
upon the horns of knowing and not knowing
what I am hearing in the silence.

I cling to having lived three decades
side by side with my best friend
but after what may happen next
silence will be hissing through the air
whenever I am brave enough to listen.

Gone are the days

Gone are the days of little jaunts and fun,
of wandering the alleys of an unknown town,
not always holding hands but close enough
to brush the fingers of my left against his right,
reminding him how much, although unsaid,
as things so often are between us,
how very much he means to me.

Gone are the cappuccino café treats
consumed in Costa on a Saturday
or sudden visits to the cinema
for films our children wouldn't think I'd like
but having gone with him to see one
so greatly fired my sense of self
that I could face the violence.

Gone are the trips across the Channel
racing to take our place upon the Shuttle,
always later than we'd planned,
adding to that sense of spontaneity,
snacking from kiosks near the queue of cars,
trying to stop my sandwich crumbs
from falling on his car's upholstery,

trying and failing so it soon became
our joke – an extra layer to the pleasure
I feel at being away from home with him
or, rather, how I used to feel
when jaunts and treats and jokes were happening.

Not falling

I tell my cat,
"Don't trip me on the stairs."
Today would be a bad day for a fall,
too much to do and far too much
is on my mind, which might
break up into a million pieces.
But really it's a perfect day to fall
when accident's the only game in town
and everywhere I look is down.

Beloved

Beloved, maybe
you won't believe this,
you with your manly way

of owning to emotion
only in so far as need be
and in monosyllables

but I, in my foolishness,
had waited half a lifetime
to hear you speak more fully

of what I meant to you
or how you felt.
Dear Heavens, even I

don't know what exactly
I wanted you to say
except that it was more.

Yet as we stare,
hand-in-hand into the abyss
and contemplate your end

your touch is telling me
more truly than romantic words,
more fully than a speech,

how you are drawn to me
as much as I to you,
that love is what you feel.

I have waited
almost all our years together,
not patiently

nor wisely either
and only now discovered
the way things are between us.

Fairy-lighted time

Indeterminate blue-green of dusk
gathers around our eucalyptus.
One plane comes into land.
Sundry stars and Venus start
to make their presence known.
Sky is the colour French would call
crepuscule. Why, knowing this,
do I persist in trying to find
a matching word in English?
Maybe to stop myself from asking
why you are going away again
for two more of the days remaining
out of our string of fairy-lighted time,
forty-eight hours of trying not to utter,
even silently, what we both know.
Hapless in its glassy prison
my heart persists in fluttering –
a lamp reluctant to illuminate.

The Hug

I heard a Buddhist say
people can be truly happy
only if they stay within the moment
long enough to know their happiness.

When your husband hugs you it feels good,
really good because, much of the time,
you and he do different things
and travel different paths.

Will you draw back and flee his hug,
this special one he's offering tonight
because he may not soon be able to,
illness having stolen him away?

Take the hug of now that feels so fine.
It's neither currency to spend nor, yet,
insurance sad times won't come back again
but it can make you happy now.

This is one whole moment of your life
when you know exactly how it feels,
and your body will remember,
being enfolded in the arms of love.

Navigation

Beside you but alone, I note your silences,
the piles of medicine covering the bed,
the look you have about your mouth
when you are speaking to me,
less often even than you used to do.
That look, the medicine and the silences
are all the navigation aids I have
to steer our ship of marriage.

Your last weeks

I won't forget the slow
shutting down of options
as cancer's blinds
slide down around you
leaving me outside.

Nor will I forget
how words abandon you,
just a few at first –
swallows in the autumn
flapping round your head,
then more of them
gathered on a wire.

Your lips struggle silently.
Your eyes ask me why
speech is being denied
as a wind, colder than before,
heralds your winter.

Holding Hands

When there seems
overwhelmingly
nothing more the doctors
feel that they can do;
when your failing strength,
inability to speak,
painfully drawn breath,
and screwed-up features
show the battle is upon you,
I hold your hands
and you grip mine.

It might be
all I have to offer
but it is what you need
for courage and for comfort
as you face moving on
from being a living human
to what might lie beyond.
Once you've gone, unequivocably,
I will let go your hands
but keep the memory of them
pressing mine.

Metamorphosis

Attached to nested tubes beside the bed
his body starts its final metamorphosis
as if he might become a dragonfly.

Having provided sturdy armour
for his existence here on Earth,
this form must now be shed.

She waits to see his wings unfurl –
as fluid fills their membranes –
and his abdomen extend.

After a painful struggle it is done.
He leaves behind the husk that held his life
and, with a farewell shimmer, he ascends.

BEREAVED

What I tell myself at night…

everything that can happen
has to happen in the day
when the school-run runs,
delivery men deliver,
phones ring, bees hum,
enough money is spent on things
(no-one really wants)
to feed a small country.

By day, I sometimes feel
I'm making progress, although
to what end I don't know.
At night, when I peel back
the purple bedroom curtains,
it's always the same sight –

the world is dark, ground wet,
no light except from street lamps.
The same rain falls each night,
keeps shining on the tarmac
making cars' reflections shiver
and traffic lights re-echo as, at night,
nothing new can happen.

It *can't* have been at night
when you found death
nor could it be so late,
a week before that, when,
frightened beyond thought,
I rushed you back to hospital.

None of what people say
or memory relates, came overnight.
It can't have done, because at night
nothing changes. The sky stays dark.
Lorries rumble anonymously from A to B.
Trees are bright-whipped wheels of twigs
going nowhere; and the rain,
ah the rain, keeps on falling.

Invisible Friend

Love, it's only me, as usual,
asking you for something.

Now your body has been turned to ash
and your voice no longer sounds around the house

will you be my best *invisible* friend?
After lights out, may I spend some time with you,

let it be our secret rendezvous?
I used to love and can't stop loving you.

Not ever being close to you again
is threatening to wrench me into two

but if you will continue as my friend
there'll still be something I can cling to –

out of reach, and out of sight and sound
but round my heart to shield me from the blues.

I planted runner beans...

ten seedlings I'd been growing on
in extra tall and narrow pots
to get a longer root run.

After soaking them twice over,
the fingers of my left hand spread
to catch each plant emerging.

As it slid out smoothly from the pot,
I felt its weight accumulate
until I cradled life within my hand;

held that seedling's whole existence,
the pairs of beans that, months from now,
would hang from it at harvest;

reminding me – hard times can help us grow,
developing our reach and strength,
rooted to support ourselves like beans.

Freezing Beans

Preparing runner beans for freezing,
a logical precise procedure –

I destring, chop and blanch,
then plunge them into icy water.

I'm working my way through them
and the kitchen's fallen silent.

The funeral's a week into my past
but still I can't make sense of things.

Last month I took him every day
for bouts of radiotherapy –

something he felt, the doctors thought
and everyone was confident would help.

I drove him extra carefully,
his balance isn't, wasn't, good those days.

He did his part, I mine, within our plan
to get his cancer to remission.

I know there was a man beside me
on every journey, never saying much

but there, someone I could smile at,
hug, see safely to a nurse's care.

Where is he, how did we get from there
to here in such a little time?

I look down at the chopping board.
It's full of scraps, dark green,
left over from the life of beans.

Guilt

So many reasons for my guilt –
      for never having said goodbye;
      for asking them to give more pain-relief
      and as they gave it, hearing you say "no"
      after you hadn't spoken for a day;
      for having hoped that kidney failure
      would take your life before
      brain cancer killed your personality;
      for illness beating all my schemes
      to get you well again –
for all of these, I daily beg
forgiveness from myself.

Don't say it

I must resist the urge to say,
"Pull yourself together, woman!"

That wouldn't match the way that Oz and I
have lived our lives.

Experience has taught me that behaviour
is rarely "always this" or "never that."

Instead our actions are the outcome
of what we've done so far
and where we're at.

If I am feeling terrible right now
it isn't that I'm failing but rather that
the challenges are greater.

Clearing out your car

With our younger daughter,
one blustery dark night,
I set to clearing out the car
you used to drive in life
before its lease expired:

stashed chocolate wrappers;
empty plastic bottles;
your old, grey, woolly hat;
flashlights everywhere,
their batteries run down.

Once we'd got it clear,
best as we could tell,
I looked across at her
bereft expression –
mirroring my own –

and said, "There's nothing else
that we can get from here,"
except our anger
that you're no longer
driving this, and sadness.

Switching off both torches
we picked up bags of rubbish
and your stuff, trudged indoors
where there were walls between
raw feelings and the wind.

Raspberries in November

Raspberries in November
glowing red as lanterns on their canes
against the darkening year,
lighting up the garden and my heart.

Amazed, I put one in my mouth,
feeling like a naughty child again
for stealing one bright moment,

as in the summer,
while you lay in bed,
too weak to join me in the garden,

I'd pick a raspberry
and try to tell you of its flavour.
There were no words to fit the way it tasted,
all I could find to say was bittersweet.

Looking forward

Looking forward to things –
storytelling, new friends or planting bulbs –
is something I can't do at present.

Getting through each day is hard enough
experts on bereavement say,
and "how-are-you?" from friends can drive me crazy.

No matter what I answer
they all go straight ahead and tell me
"There's no right way of grieving."

I mustn't blame myself for feeling
or even for not feeling over-much,
for thinking or not thinking of his touch,

the jokes I'd grown accustomed to
that oiled my daily life,
the gentle state of being his wife.

I don't know how I am
or when I will feel able to respond
to what might seem a simple question.

At least I've started to imagine
a time, however distant,
when I'll be looking forward
to my life again.

Wizard in the shed

"Hallo, the Shed"
is what I used to say
on entering your space

I having

climbed the attic stairs
got out of breath
to see you there,

beard my lion in his den
my IT handyperson in his shed
out of my depth

and you

tucked behind your screens
in between vertiginous
heaps of PC spares

and papers piled so high
all of which you meant to sign
when the time was right

oh, my darling friend

in the daily run of things
we sometimes got frustrated
with each other's differences.

I used to joke about you in your shed,
spending family time on PC networks
or chatting worldwide on the web.
At least you were right there.

My loss

My one fixed point,
my reference library
on anything and everything
I wished to know,
my wisest friend,

my confidence
your answers would contain
no self-aggrandisement
or jokes at my expense,
those flaws weren't in you,

but all my trust that you and I
would just continue on
has now been lost.

Something I don't know

The sky between the fence and tree
is still the same sky I would comment on
while sitting opposite your chair
if we had planned to take a walk
or yesterday I'd sown some seeds –
happy inconsequential talk.

I'd wait for you to check your phone
and share the weather for today,
or mention that a NASA probe
would circle Mars within the week,
telling me something I don't know,
or didn't then.

It is the same sky but your share
now rests within my awkward hands.
You, who were always well informed,
who read voraciously, whose words
were few but funny, wise and kind,
are gone.

Now I hold up the sky for you
and marvel at the sunset glow
or strands of cloud like herring bones,
and, during lightning, guard the cats,
but all alone with no-one here
to tell me something I don't know.

AFTER-KNOWLEDGE

A widow's words to her counsellor

Somehow I doubt you'll get the truth
or to the heart of what
there was between us while he lived –

the up and down of passing days,
those last few dozen that we had,
my pleasure in arranging trays

of breakfast near his end-of-life,
the few foods he still liked,
and watching them consumed

then washing up the spoon and knife
for use the following day,
the thought that there would be such days,

a thought that now I've lost or shed
to stop myself being caught with tears
and sole survivor's grief.

But if, upon the talking journey, we
discuss that long-gone moment when
he gently ran a warm shower over me
to wash the strain of childbirth off;

or at the other end of life
he loved enough to buy a gift for me
(just found with Christmas wrapping in the loft)
to fiddle with (my hands are never still)

the thrill of seeing that he'd thought of me,
even if illness caught him out too soon
and he forgot to give me this small toy,
he gave me daily, over years, such joy.

This truth is what I hope you'll help me see,
like other widows whom you've spoken to
and widowers. It seems as if it's often we,
women, who cling to life tenaciously;

though why we do when being left alone
hurts like a splinter that extends
until the skin's no thicker than a hair
around its pain, why still survive?

                                        But then,
he would have given anything for longer life
if that had been within the doctors' gift or mine.

Hindsight

I'm looking back
through the smudged lens
of recollection
at a couple waiting for a train,
two people out of thousands
visiting Zadar that afternoon.

And my heart aches
with after-knowledge
of symptoms you concealed,
postponing treatment,
leading to this point, one year on,
when I'm alone.

What if I went back,
and wrote a message in the sand
warning that you might not make it,
but then we could have lost
our final holiday together,
our year of living hopefully,

and you might still have died.

My bedroom…

piece by piece restored
to a semblance of order,
how it was before
or I wanted it to seem,

photos in their albums,
sheets and carpets clean,
books ranged on shelves,
out of harm's way.

Order, always I search
for what is neater,
more easily controlled
but underneath's a storm –

grief hawks through my soul;
tension racks my bones;
beneath me, ground falls away
into loneliness.

Goodbye

As I wake
the knowledge spills its ink
right over me,
a spreading blot of panic,
guilt, unhappiness.

Five months now
since I held your hand
and felt the loving pressure
of those precious fingers
but did I say goodbye?

In last night's film
a couple knew
they had to part
because the husband
was about to die.

Standing very close,
her hand upon his cheek,
her speech, scripted
and rehearsed, no doubt,
a dozen times,

but still,
it shook the fabric
of the world I've built –
tidy, busy, purposeful –
ever since your death.

Did we not realise
in those last fevered weeks
how deep a need I had
for us to say goodbye
so I could start preparing
to let you go?

Phone call from a friend

He rang to tell me of her death,
"Only last night, in my arms.
At the end she felt no pain."

I listened to familiar phrases,
heard his voice shake,
and thought of you –
at the end not in my arms,
for fear of fouling tubes
or catching bruises –
for whom I begged more pain relief
when you could not, yourself,
having lost speech;

thought of you
softer-edged and greyer
on a stretcher trolley
pressing its plastic side;
your tree-trunk felled;
then lighter – a sycamore key
or far-flying flake of ash
blown beyond a bonfire
to settle who knows where.

At both ends of the phone-line
throats were burning.
He offered comfort for my loss
as I was struggling for words
to do the same for him,
each wishing that our flakes of ash
had ceased their whirling
and come back,
each of us wishing,

while ash that we'll in turn become
swirls around some future fire
years or months from now.

Your turn to cook

Love, I used to hear you
rattling the dishes, slicing things.
Perhaps you didn't know
how much I liked to listen
to your rare cooking in the kitchen.
Downstairs and at the end
of our untidy corridor,
still I could hear you swish
those crafty cooking tools –
the owl-hoot flip of spatula
through frying onions, and the sizzle
of absurd amounts of butter,
the pouring out of your continual
milk of human kindness –
so generous, and a sense
of something very special being made –
your love preparing itself,
always there for me,
even at those moments like today,
when I no longer hear you.

Six months on

Today I took a photo
from its hiding place
and put it on display,
seeing those in it, you and I,
as if we were sweet strangers –
three years ago on the London Eye,
smiles full-moon strength
to celebrate our anniversary
and marvel at how far we'd come.

Little did I know,
as I thanked the woman
who had held the camera,
how far we'd yet to go.
but I still bear the imprint
of how I felt that evening.

As I lean in to kiss the photo
and wonder when my lips
will wear right through
the glass between us,
a flicker of your presence
hangs about the recollection
helping me address
this milestone
and others yet to come.

Whereabouts unknown

You are with the dead, my love,
maybe on the ground in Richmond Park,
one with your ashes where we scattered them,
in bracken, round the roots of trees, among
the fallen leaves and beetle skeletons.

You are with the dead, on Earth
or in the spiritual aether others speak of
but I have only ever half-believed in.
My messages to you are one-way now.
However much I say, you don't reply.

Despite the hiss and crackle of self-doubt
it seems essential to keep telling you
about our children and the planet,
and though I do not hear your answer
I send my love and sense that someone,
my special someone, has been listening.

A year of getting ready…

to move
and lose the relative
security of being here

to pack
the most important things
are not in boxes

Moving Day

I look ahead to moving day –
my clothes already packed,
his books gone to a college,
plant pots in the car
driven by a daughter,
cats safely with my son.

Keys gripped in my right hand
I'm standing at the door,
poised to leave this house
for a much smaller one
I hope will suit me better.
There's just one problem –

I don't know who I am,
not anymore. Once I was a girl,
then a woman married and divorced,
married again and widowed,
Now, not knowing who or what to be
is troubling me.

When I'm ready

If and when I'm ready
to listen to the slow dark tick
of minutes after midnight
without impatience;
and not to shrink away
from ambulances' sudden wails
or groaning cars that pass here
on their lonely journeys home;
and when it's possible to bear
the shriek of wind in branches
leafless after days of winter rain,
then maybe I'll be ready too
to meet you smiling
in my dreams again.

Go on, fill your boots!

Beyond the bathroom window
lies our wild, wet garden
but also, the wider world
full of nature and people –
themselves a part of nature –
and, hopefully, adventures.

I mean to fill my boots
with everything I can:
friends and late-night drinks,
poetry events, walks in wild places,
over-generous helpings
of cream cakes, curry and Rosé;

to travel further than was planned,
climb higher than I used to dare,
speak up when challenged
and champion the oppressed,
look out and down across new lands,
or even down-and-out, who cares?

Outside the bathroom window
on its mortared sill,
a rubber pump is lying,
part of the water-saving system
my husband built for me
while his hands still could.

Hesitantly I stroke
the pump's dark surface,
which for an instant feels
like someone's palm,
firm and slightly warm,
held out to steady me.

How I wish, even while I know
dry winds of seven months' winter
and the hailstorm yesterday
must have removed all trace,
but how I wish for contact.
Still, there's nothing for it,
people and nature wait,
I'll fill my boots.

Footnote: *"Fill your boots" is to get as much as you can of something valuable or desirable*

St Bees Beach

St Bees Beach in Cumbria,
visited with my younger daughter
on what was once her father's birthday;

sky threatening more rain, and grey
water heaving dispiritedly against
a shore of steep-shelved pebbles.

I couldn't see the beauty of it
even though the red cliffs in the distance
were said to be beloved by seabirds

and the pebbles, turning out to be
so many colours, made it hard to know
which ones to carry home,

but still it was a disappointment.
Our special day remembering the man
felt thwarted before it had begun.

Unwilling to go back without, at least,
one new-made memory, we chose to walk
the first part of the Coast-to-Coast,

over the little wooden bridge
and up the limestone cliff.
But as, quite silently, we trudged

tangled dune and streamside plants
gave way to a glorious profusion
of minute downland blossoms

buffeted and rustling in the wind,
pink and purple, ochre and brilliant blue
framing a maritime horizon.

She and I, climbing higher still;
an ebbing tide revealing golden sands
with children splashing through the shallows

and more children arriving on school buses,
their tiny, high-vis jerkins flowering,
sudden as Welsh poppies far below;

then June sun coming out
and, if only for a moment,
finding myself again
feeling happy.

CAMILLA REEVE - BIOGRAPHY

Camilla Reeve is a writer, independent publisher and organic gardener camilla_reeve@yahoo.co.uk. She has four previous poetry collections: *Travels of a Spider,* 2006; *Travelling East by Road and Soul,* (flipped eye publishing) 2009; *Raft of Puffins,* 2016; and *Tales from Two Cities,* 2018; and enjoys performing her work live. Her YA futuristic fantasy, *The Cloud Singer,* is about global warming and she is working on its sequel. In 2016, after 30 years in IT, she founded Palewell Press, publishing books on Justice, Equality and Sustainability https://www.palewellpress.co.uk. Palewell Press is a founding member of the Changing Wor(l)ds Network of cultural activists.

www.ingramcontent.com/pod-product-compliance
Lightning Source LLC
Chambersburg PA
CBHW070334120526
44590CB00017B/2884